The After-School Alien Club

Jonny Zucker

Illustrated by Aleksei Bitskoff

Contents

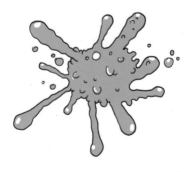

OXFORD
UNIVERSITY PRESS

The Mighty Blam Battle

Everyone at Amber Primary School wanted to go to the after-school club. It was just like a normal club ... except that it was run by aliens!

The aliens were called Tap and Kod. They had come to Earth from their home planet to live with the humans. Tap had gigantic ears which he used like hands. Kod had a nose which was so strong she could pick up a child with it!

One afternoon, Rick, Bella and their friends ran into the club hut. Their head teacher, Mr Keys, was talking to Tap.

'Your club makes too much mess!' said Mr Keys.

'But mess is fun!' replied Tap, patting Mr Keys on the back with one of his giant ears.

'Any more mess and I will close this club down!' said Mr Keys, stomping off.

The children were worried.

'Will he close down the club?' asked Bella.

'No way!' laughed Kod. 'We can tidy up later.' She took a shiny orange thing from a box. 'This is a Blam alien,' she said.

'Hi!' grinned the little Blam. Kod pulled the Blam's ear. A glob of orange goo shot across and landed on Tap's head.

'Hey!' yelled Tap. 'I wasn't ready for that!'

Kod took lots
more Blams out of
the box. Tap gave
everyone a silver
flying suit.

'Who wants a Blam
fight?' asked Kod. 'Me
and Tap against you lot!'

'Yay!' everyone cheered.

'Game on!' shouted Tap.

Rick zoomed into the air and flicked
his Blam's ear. Soon everyone was covered
in goo – and so was the room!

'This is awesome!' cried Rick, as he splattered Kod's back.

'Brilliant!' cried Bella. But then she looked out of the window and gulped. 'Mr Keys is coming!' she yelled.

'Quick!' screamed Tap. 'Everyone tidy up!'

There was a mad scramble. Bella and Rick collected the Blams. The others started chucking goo into the dustbin. Tap swept the floor with his ears.

But they weren't quick enough. When Mr Keys charged in, there was still orange goo everywhere.

'This is the end of the club,' whispered Bella.

'WHAT IS
GOING ON?'
thundered Mr Keys.
'It's ... it's
Orange Goo Day!'
spluttered Tap.

Mr Keys picked up
a Blam. 'What does
this do?' he asked.

Kod flicked the
Blam's ear and some
orange goo landed
on Mr Keys' chin.

'Oh no!'
gasped Rick,
but Mr Keys
was ... smiling!

'This looks
like ... *fun*,' said
Mr Keys. 'Can I
have a go?'

'Of course!'
grinned Tap, throwing
Mr Keys a flying suit. 'You can be
on the children's side!'

'Are you going to close down the club?'
asked Bella, still feeling worried.

'Not if you play games like
this!' laughed Mr Keys.
And just to prove it, he
zoomed up and shot a
big glob of goo, right at
Kod's head.

The Intergalactic Shopping Trip

One day at the after-school club, Rick was unhappy because one of the bikes was broken. 'The best bike is mashed!' he said.

'What a shame,' said Kod.

'Can you fix it?' asked Rick.

'Not now,' said Tap. 'We're going on an intergalactic ingredients shopping trip!'

Oh no! thought Rick. *Last time we did that, Tap and Kod made horrible exploding pancakes*!

'Everyone into the spaceship!' called Kod.

Rick, Bella and the others climbed inside the spaceship.

'Hold on tight!' called Tap.

The spaceship shot upwards at an incredible speed. Soon they were millions of miles into outer space.

Finally they reached Tap and Kod's home planet. Kod flicked a switch and everyone whizzed through a hole in the spaceship's roof. They landed with a bump on a soft purple field.

'First we need two Goob snakes,' said Kod.

Bella spotted some slithery pink snakes with long silver tongues.

'Don't worry,' said Tap. 'They won't hurt you.'

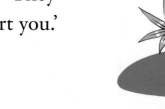

'Er ... OK,' said Bella. She carefully picked up two snakes and gave them to Kod.

'Yuck!' said Rick. 'I'm not eating snakes!'

'Now we need some branches from that Corsack tree,' said Tap.

At the end of the field was a very thin tree with glowing, light-blue branches. When the children got near the tree, it screamed and ran off.

The children chased it round the field.

'We only want four branches!' shouted Tap, leaping at the tree and pulling it to the ground with his giant ears.

'Well, why didn't you say so?' said the tree. It threw four branches into the air. Rick caught two and his friends Yaz and Carl caught the others.

'Last, we need a Vecca rock,' said Kod.
She pointed at some red and white rocks
that were bouncing up and down very
quickly. Bella grabbed one.

'That's all the ingredients!' shouted
Kod. 'Everyone back in the spaceship!'

When they got back to the club, Tap and the children played cricket outside. Kod went inside with the ingredients.

'I bet she's making some horrible alien soup,' Rick whispered to Bella.

Half an hour later, Kod called Rick inside.

Oh no! he thought. *She's going to make me taste the soup*! But he was wrong. Kod had made a new bike from the Goob snakes and Corsack branches!

'Awesome!' said Rick. 'Does it go fast?'

'Try it!' laughed Kod.

Rick took the bike outside and started pedalling. 'It's not very fast,' he complained.

'Hang on,' said Kod, sticking the Vecca rock on to the frame. 'This will make it go a bit faster!'

For a few seconds, nothing happened.

'It doesn't work!' moaned Rick.

Suddenly there was a loud BANG and the bike shot forwards.

'This is amazing!' yelled Rick, holding on tightly.

'Oh no! I forgot something!' shouted Kod.

'What was it?' shouted Rick.

'The *brakes*!' roared Kod, as Rick disappeared into the distance.

Alien Shakes

It was snack time at the After-School Alien Club. Kod tipped two zog-mud slime balls and some alien nettles into a jug. She whisked it up with her nose until it hissed and gurgled.

'Try this ultra-tasty alien shake,' said Kod, pouring the mixture into cups.

Tap slurped his happily. Rick, Bella and the others took small sips.

'Eurrrggghhhh!' cried Rick. 'That's disgusting!'

Just then, Mr Keys burst into the hut.

'Have an alien shake,' offered Kod.

'It looks ... er ... delicious,' replied Mr Keys, 'but we're playing a football match against Greenway Primary and our best player has just been injured.'

'Can I play?' asked Tap, hopefully.

'Thanks, but no,' said Mr Keys. 'I want Rick to play.'

Tap looked very disappointed.

Kod grabbed Rick with her nose and flung him towards the school building. He ran in and got changed in record time. When Rick got to the pitch, everyone from the after-school club was there to cheer him on.

'Go, Rick!' yelled Tap, jumping up and down.

'It's 2–1 to Amber Primary,' announced Mr Keys. 'There's ten minutes to go!' He blew his whistle.

Rick ran towards the ball. He kicked it but slipped and fell to the ground. He cried out and clutched his foot. He had twisted his ankle!

'I don't believe this!' groaned Mr Keys. Bella helped Rick off the field.

'Have no fear, Mr Keys!' shouted Tap.
He reached into his left ear. He kept a
football kit in there, just in case. Before
Mr Keys could stop him, Tap was changed
and on the pitch.

Tap whacked the ball so hard it disappeared over the horizon. Luckily there was a spare ball. Tap balanced it on his chin and ran towards his own goal.

'Stop!' screamed the Amber players, but Tap threw himself and the ball into the net.

'Goal!' yelled the Greenway players.

'That's 2–2 with six minutes to go!'
shouted Mr Keys.

Just then, Bella had an idea. She raced
back to the club hut and grabbed a cup
of alien shake. When she got back to the
match, Tap was heading towards the Amber
goal again.

Bella ran behind the Greenway goal and held up the cup of alien shake. 'Hey, Tap!' she shouted. 'Come and get this!'

Tap looked at the frothing shake. 'Tasty!' he shouted.

With the ball at his feet, Tap zoomed down the pitch. He fired the ball into the Greenway goal and crashed through the net to grab the cup. He took a big gulp.

'Game over!' shouted Mr Keys. 'It's 3–2 to Amber Primary!'

'Tap is our hero!' yelled the Amber players.

'Here's a prize for being such a good referee,' said Tap, offering the rest of his shake to Mr Keys.

'Er ... no, thank you,' said Mr Keys, edging away quickly.

'Wait!' cried Tap, running after him. 'You said it looked delicious!'

About the author

I am the award-winning author of the *Monster Swap* series (with Tony Ross) and the *Striker Boy* and *Max Flash* series. I love writing about football and magic, and particularly enjoy writing funny stories. Each year I visit loads of schools, teaching children that writing can be fun!

When I was a teacher I organized an after-school club and often wondered what it would be like if aliens flew down to help me run it! It was this crazy thought that inspired me to write *The After-School Alien Club*.